gs

Brisbane

laide

Sydney

Canberra

ourne

Hobart

To Uncle Peter,

A reminder of your
trip to Australia,

Love,

Carl

Dec '96

AUSTRALIA

A POCKET BOOK

PHOTOGRAPHY BY GARY LEWIS

AUSTRALIA

A POCKET BOOK

Australia a Pocket Book comprises a unique collection of photographs from the camera of Gary Lewis, one of Australia's foremost photographers.

Australia is a land of richly varied landscapes, vivid colours and striking contrasts. From the dry scorched deserts of the red centre to the tranquil beauty of its tropical islands, Australia displays a breathtaking diversity.

The world's only island continent is geologically ancient; its two hundred years of European settlement a brief chapter of history in contrast to its 40,000 years of Aboriginal heritage.

As in no other country, visitors to Australia can enjoy a wide variety of landscapes and experiences; from its tropical rainforests to its vast snowfields, unique wildlife and ultra-modern cities. You can marvel at the breathtaking views from its majestic mountain summits, to the unparalleled beauty of the longest coral reef chain in the world.

Whilst no single book could hope to capture all of Australia's incredible secrets, *Australia a Pocket Book* remains a wonderful memento and record of time spent, places visited and experiences enjoyed.

Aboriginal rock paintings, Kakadu, Northern Territory

Aboriginal rock paintings, Kakadu, Northern Territory

Olgas, Northern Territory

Sunset, Olgas, Northern Territory

Wave Rock, Hyden, Western Australia

King's Canyon, Northern Territory

Katherine Gorge, lower reaches, Northern Territory

Jedda Rock, Katherine Gorge, Northern Territory

Climbing face, Uluru (Ayers Rock), Northern Territory

Sunrise, aerial view, Uluru (Ayers Rock), Northern Territory

Iron ore country, Western Australia

The Macdonnell Ranges, Northern Territory

Hardy's Reef, Great Barrier Reef, Queensland

Low Island, Great Barrier Reef, Queensland

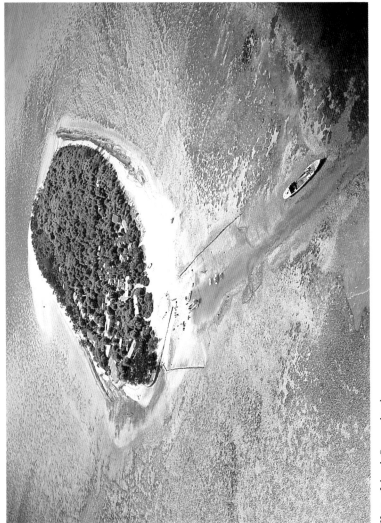

Heron Island, Queensland

Lizard Island, far north Queensland

Cedar Bay, Cooktown, Queensland

Hinchinbrook Island, Whitsundays, Queensland

Whitsunday sunset from South Molle Island, Queensland

Late afternoon, Whitsunday Passage, Queensland

Philip Island coastline, Victoria

Basalt cliffs, Tasman Island

Binnaburra, southern Queensland

Towards Mt. William, western Victoria

Mt. Lyell, Queenstown, south-west Tasmania

Mt. Roland, northern Tasmania

Thredbo, southern New South Wales

Bogong High Plains, from the Ovens River, Victoria

Lyell Highway, southern Tasmania

Mt. Nelson, south-west Tasmania

Fern gully, Dandenong Ranges, Victoria

Tree-fern, Dandenong Ranges, Victoria

Mt. Tambourine, southern Queensland

Fraser Island, Queensland

Hydrofoil, Sydney Harbour, New South Wales (no longer in use)

Sydney Tower at night, Sydney, New South Wales

Sunset over the Westgate Bridge, Melbourne, Victoria

Evening along St. Kilda Road, Melbourne, Victoria

Market Day, Salamanca Place, Hobart, Tasmania

Hobart and the Tasman Bridge, Tasmania

Colonel Light and city skyline, Adelaide, South Australia

Rundle Street Mall, Adelaide, South Australia

Multicultural Fremantle, Western Australia

Perth skyline at night, Western Australia

Todd River race, Alice Springs, Northern Territory

The city of Darwin, Northern Territory

Story Bridge, Brisbane, Queensland

Town Hall, Brisbane, Queensland

The new Parliament House, Australian Capital Territory

Capital Hill from Mt. Ainslie, Australian Capital Territory

Sheep droving, New South Wales

Cattle mustering, north east Victoria

Country mailboxes, north east Victoria

Sheep grazing, central New South Wales

Morning mists, Myrtleford, north-eastern Victoria

Water pump and outbuildings, southern Queensland

Koala

Echidna

Emu

Kangaroo

Platypus

Warrnambool, western Victoria

Wattle

Kangaroo Paw

Wombat

River estuary, Flinders Island

Kiewa River, Harrietville, north-east Victoria

Derwent River, Tasmania

Hogarth Falls, Strahan, south-west Tasmania

Mountfield National Park, southern Tasmania

Floods, Mackay, Queensland

Ox-bow lakes, Mackay, Queensland

Mt. Murchison Lake, southern Tasmania

Mitchell River, Cairns, Queensland

Port Arthur, penal settlement, Tasmania

Shot tower, Hobart, Tasmania

First published in Australia in 1993 by
Gary Allen Pty Ltd
9 Cooper Street
Smithfield NSW 2164

Designed and produced by Allan Cornwell
Typeset by Half A Sec, Frankston, Victoria
Produced by Mandarin Offset in Hong Kong

Photographs © Gary Lewis
ISBN 1-875169-30-X